Unfinished Business

The miners' strike for jobs 1984-5

Peter Arkell & Ray Rising

a world to win

for a future without global capitalism

Published by Lupus Books
PO Box 942
London SW1V 2AR

www.aworldtowin.net
info@aworldtowin.net
07871 745258

ISBN 978-0-9523454-6-6

Cover design Nick Feldman
Design and typography by Robbie Griffiths

Printed on FSC certified paper
Printed and bound by CPI Antony Rowe
Chippenham Wiltshire SN14 6LH

FSC
Mixed Sources
Product group from well-managed
forests and other controlled sources
Cert no. SGS-COC-2953
www.fsc.org
© 1996 Forest Stewardship Council

Contents

Photos by Peter Arkell, Ray Rising, Sean Smith and Katalin Arkell

Introduction

THE 1984-5 MINERS' STRIKE AGAINST PIT CLOSURES was the longest national dispute in British history, and one of the most decisive. Near civil war conditions prevailed in mining communities as the forces of the state descended on pit villages. Vast numbers of police prevented striking miners from moving around the country and smashed mass pickets like those mounted at Orgreave.

By rejecting the decision of the Thatcher government and the state-controlled National Coal Board to close pits that were deemed "uneconomic", the miners challenged the very basis of the capitalist system of production. The miners' insistence on jobs and communities coming before profit was rejected outright by the Tories, who mobilised the state in an unprecedented way.

Thatcher's government that came to power in 1979 immediately pursued a series of aggressive shock measures in order to break the resistance of the trade unions and the working class. Her agenda was clear: to impose a new type of ruthless, free-market capitalism in Britain and to open the path to corporate-driven globalisation.

The year-long strike, which took place during a serious recession, marked the moment when the plans of the government finally collided with the expectations of the masses. Miners answered the challenge of history, turned and fought back, in the reasonable hope and expectation of uniting all workers against the policies of mass unemployment, privatisation and poverty. The miners' strike for jobs inspired everyone who took part: the miners themselves, most of them young, their wives and the women of the coalfields, whose outlook was transformed in the course of the year, and the hundreds of thousands all over the country who supported the strike actively.

At the start, the National Union of Mineworkers, led by Arthur Scargill, unleashed a huge blast of energy from the rank-and-file and their supporters in other unions. Gradually, however, the strike became more and more isolated and eventually turned into a grim struggle for survival. Responsibility for this rests entirely with the Trades Union Congress leaders and the Labour Party under Neil Kinnock. They considered the strike an embarrassment and a challenge to their personal authority. Union leaders by and large sat on their hands, doing little or nothing by way of meaningful support, and presided over a betrayal more blatant, more calculated even than the sell-out in the 1926 General Strike.

Unfinished Business is not written as a reminiscence on the 25th anniversary of the start of the strike, or to marvel at the courage of the miners, although no one who lived through the struggle could dispute that. Instead our book is intended to draw out the essence of the miners' strike for jobs and its enduring significance for a new period of history. We are also publishing a series of photographs, some for the very first time, taken by us and others that show the extraordinary character of the strike.

The story and lessons of the strike are thrown into sharp relief by an immeasurably more serious global crisis of capitalist society, following the financial meltdown. Once again jobs are disappearing by the tens of thousands in Britain, while trade and manufacturing is collapsing across the world. Governments have desperately tried to re-start the capitalist economy by bailing out the very banks that share responsibility for the crisis. Ordinary working people rightly remain suspicious and hostile to these kinds of measures because they leave the rich and the powerful untouched.

Now that the economic and financial crash is joined by a deep political crisis within the British state, the opportunities are present for picking up where the miners were forced to leave off. Their insistence in 1984-5 on placing social needs before profit is just as critical and essential a quarter of a century later. Miners showed that workers will fight for an alternative to the wilful destruction of jobs and communities by capitalism if they have a firm and principled leadership. Our challenge today is to build a movement that will complete the unfinished business of the miners' strike.

Peter Arkell & Ray Rising, July 2009
News Line photographers during the 1984-5 strike

1

Provocation and confrontation

THE GOVERNMENT OF MARGARET THATCHER that won the 1979 general election was unlike previous post-war Tory governments. It came to power determined to stabilise the economy, face down the power of the trade unions and create a modernised type of ruthless capitalism in Britain.

Up until this time, it had been an agreed, if unwritten, principle shared by all the political parties that the economy should be regulated by the state. A large proportion of Britain's economy was state owned, with private industry relatively feeble. Successive governments since the end of the Second World War had followed the line of expanding the British economy within a controlled inflationary boom internationally. But in 1971, President Nixon signalled the end of the deal struck at Bretton Woods in 1944, under which currencies were tied to the dollar, which in turn was convertible into gold. Inflation took off and the leaders of world capitalism were driven into crisis.

Industrial militancy accompanied the abrupt ending of the long post-war economic boom. By the 1970s, the British unions had become very powerful. They had over 12 million members, representing more than half of the working population. The ruling classes were shocked and dismayed by their inability to bring the unions to heel. Shop stewards and rank-and-file workers, rather than union leaders, led and carried forward many of the strikes and actions. The anti-union legislation brought in by Edward Heath's Tory government addressed this issue by holding the unions responsible for the actions of their members. But these laws were blown apart in 1972 by the response to the arrest of five dockers who were thrown into Pentonville jail for picketing in defiance of the new laws. Heath found himself facing a general strike as workers around Britain struck in support of the dockers, and the courts were compelled to find a way of releasing the dockers without delay.

Then later in 1972 a pay strike by the National Union of Mineworkers (NUM) forced Heath into a humiliating surrender. Two years later in 1974, a second miners' strike had even more dramatic results. On 7 February 1974, Heath called a snap election in the middle of the strike on the question of "Who rules Britain?". He narrowly lost the election, as voters backed the miners. In March, the Labour government that took office settled the strike on the miners' terms and proved unable to rein in the militancy of the workers. Battered by the economic crisis, Labour was eventually forced to go cap in hand to the International Monetary Fund. It was defeated in the 1979 election after a "Winter of Discontent" of public sector pay strikes.

Meanwhile, a significant section of the Tory party, including Thatcher herself, who had replaced Heath as leader in February 1975, embraced the ideas of Milton Friedman and the Chicago School of economists. They had developed monetarist, free-market policies that were aimed at freeing capitalism from regulation and control. Friedman's policies were first implemented in Chile after the 1973 US-organised coup overthrew the Allende government and replaced it with the Pinochet military dictatorship.

The coming to power of Thatcher in Britain quickly followed by Reagan in America, meant that the major capitalist economies would soon be subjected to monetarist trial by fire. One of the first acts of the Thatcher government was to abolish controls on currency exchange. Mass unemployment, the promotion of the "ownership society" and of individualism, attacks on local government, a pointed hostility to negotiating any compromises with the unions, a refusal to rescue any ailing industry, a contempt for society as a whole unless it was subordinate to the interests of the profit makers – all these policies and ideas were soon brought out into the open and aggressively pursued by the new Tory government.

Unemployment rose to 3.25 million by 1981 and stayed at around that level for five years. But the working class remained militant and undefeated and Thatcher needed to put the unions firmly in their place as part of her plan to make capitalism in Britain a place safe for corporate and financial interests. The Tory party leaders had reflected long and hard on how this might be done. A showdown with the working class became inevitable.

Preparing for a showdown

In 1974, Tory MP Nicholas Ridley, a founding member of the right-wing Selsdon Group of free market Conservatives, drew up a report on the nationalised industries. Ridley proposed how the next Conservative government could fight and defeat a major strike in a nationalised industry. He plainly had the miners in mind when he recommended that coal stocks should be built up at power stations and plans made to import coal from non-union foreign ports. He advocated the recruitment of non-union drivers by haulage companies and the conversion of power stations to burn both coal and oil.

Ridley recommended that social security payments for strikers' families should be cut and that a large mobile squad of police be trained and equipped in riot control to uphold the law against "violent picketing". In short, he drew up a plan to re-tool the forces of the state. Ridley also urged the government to choose the field and the timing of the battle if at all possible. The incoming Thatcher government adopted all these proposals. In addition, the government strengthened the anti-union laws, directing the MI5 secret police to snoop, spy and bug the labour movement and the Left. Agents and informers were placed in and around the NUM and socialist political organisations. At the same time, the Tories cultivated the leaders of the EEPTU electricians' union, the steelworkers' leaders and other "moderate" unions.

By contrast with the Tories, the Trades Union Congress and most of the union leaders had learnt little or nothing of importance from the events of the 1970s or from the first three years of Tory rule. Despite the arrival on the scene of a new kind of government, they carried on with old habits, simply reacting to events, but foreseeing nothing and planning less. Any notion of a co-ordinated programme of resistance by all the unions was never on the agenda. Before 1979, governments were always summoning the TUC leaders to Downing Street in order to bring them, nominally at least, into the business of governing. Now they were out in the cold.

As for the Labour Party, under Neil Kinnock's leadership since 1983, the last thing it was preparing to do was to mount any effective resistance to the policies of mass unemployment and the wholesale destruction of industry being pursued by the Tory government. Kinnock instead launched a campaign against the so-called "hard left" in the party. His crusade to "modernise" the party was really nothing more than an adaptation to Thatcherism, in order to create a new kind of Labour Party free of socialist policies and safe for big business. Kinnock, a miners' son himself, was to become a bitter opponent of the strike.

The miners alone stood in the way of the Tories, with the TUC, most of the unions and the Labour Party paralysed and awe-struck in the face of the attack on jobs and communities. The NUM could be counted on not to buckle. The miners were buoyed by their two victories in the 1970s, the second of which in 1974 had brought down Heath's Tories. They were viewed rightly as the bedrock of the British labour movement, had strength in numbers, a long commitment to socialism and form on the battlefield. And, from 1982, they were led by the plain-speaking, charismatic Arthur Scargill, who on numerous occasions had expressed his contempt for Thatcherism and everything it stood for.

Miners had fought for and in 1947 celebrated the nationalisation of the coal industry by the Atlee government in. But while working conditions improved and the hated owners were removed, there was no question of miners actually controlling the industry. The new, unelected board managed and ran the coal industry, with its dependence on government subsidies. The National Coal Board (NCB) absorbed the debt of £358 million paid to the old owners in compensation. There was a shortage of money for investment in new machines and technology. Historically the coal industry had been in slow decline since 1913, when there were 1,250,000 miners. Yet even in 1957 there were still 700,000 miners producing 220 million tons of coal a year. But throughout the late 1950s and the 1960s, the rate of pit closures accelerated sharply leading to the loss of half the workforce in less than 15 years. The NUM, then under the leadership of Arthur Horner and Will Paynter, both members of the Communist Party, offered little resistance.

The election of the Labour government of Harold Wilson in 1964 brought no respite. On the contrary, in the four years from 1965 to 1969 over 200 pits were closed. By the time of the 1972 strike, the number of miners had fallen to 320,000. The incoming 1974 Labour government introduced the *Plan for Coal*, with the aim of expanding the industry through a huge investment programme, but this was not fully implemented and the nuclear option took priority, along with North Sea oil.

With the fall of Labour in 1979 and the election of the Thatcher government with its strategy of undermining the coal industry, the countdown to confrontation began. In 1984, around 80% of Britain's electricity was still generated from domestic coal, and Thatcher's government was determined to sever this dependence by promoting nuclear power, oil and gas as alternative fuels – at enormous public expense. In 1981, the annual state subsidy to the industry amounted to around £680 million, far too high in the view of a government that believed only in the markets. In fact at £3.2 per ton, the subsidy was by far the lowest in West Europe. In February 1981, David Howell, the Energy Minister, promptly cut the coal subsidy, forcing the NCB to draw up a programme of closures.

The NUM reacted sharply, giving the government a week to withdraw the cuts and reinstate the full subsidy or face industrial action. Joe Gormley, then NUM president, warned miners not to strike without a ballot because of the danger of the NCB suing the union and claiming damages. But this was ignored and within a few days half the miners were on strike, including many in the moderate area of Nottinghamshire. The government's preparations proved inadequate, however. Coal stocks at the power stations were low and the government was intensely unpopular in the country. It was in no position to take on the miners in the middle of winter. To the surprise of many, the government executed a U-turn, withdrawing the proposals and promising to refer future plans for pit closures to the established review procedure. It was a "body-swerve", as the Scottish miners' leader Mick McGahey aptly called the climb-down. Soon afterwards, Arthur Scargill, the president of the Yorkshire miners, succeeded Gormley as president of the national union.

Thatcher, emboldened by the victory over Argentina in the Falklands War in 1982 and her re-election a year later, redoubled preparations for a confrontation with the miners. In 1983, the government installed the 70-year-old Ian MacGregor as the chairman of the NCB, to a chorus of anger by all the unions and even opposition within the NCB. Until his appointment, the NCB prided itself on its close ties with the miners, creating a kind of community of the whole industry, with ex-miners taking some of the top jobs at Hobart House, the NCB's London HQ.

MacGregor had earned a reputation as an industrial relations fixer in the US where he headed up a multi-national metals and mining company called Amax. After brief spells in banking and at British Leyland, he became chairman of British Steel, earning a reputation as "the butcher of the steel industry" when he oversaw nearly 100,000 redundancies between 1979 and 1983. With his hatred of organised labour and his oft-repeated mantra that management must have the right to manage, he appeared the Tories' ideal candidate to lead the war against the miners. MacGregor's outlook in 1984, echoing that of the government, was that coal production must be brought into line with what could be sold on the market. If imported American or Australian coal was cheaper, then either the cost of mining coal in Britain would have to come down or pits would need to close. He wanted to be able to close the most uneconomic pits to improve the bottom line and to reduce the subsidy.

The NUM's outlook was precisely the opposite of this. Coal, said the NUM, was a national asset and should be mined anyway, and could even be given away to help pensioners or provide cheap electricity when market conditions resulted in a surplus. Scargill told a Parliamentary select committee that coal should be mined even if it resulted in a net financial loss. The NUM maintained that pits should only be closed on grounds of exhaustion of the coal or on safety grounds. To concede the right to close uneconomic pits was to open the door to the possibility of mass closures.

On the eve of the 1984 strike, although cheaper oil from the Middle East and nuclear power had weakened the position of coal somewhat, about 180,000 miners were still producing 105 million tons of coal a year. Worried about the growing mountains of coal at the power stations, the NUM had begun an effective overtime ban in the autumn of 1983, which started to reduce the stockpiles. The government decided it was in a position to fulfil one of the main proposals of the Ridley Plan: to choose the timing of the battle.

13

The provocation – miners launch their strike

Demand for coal was falling away as winter gave way to the spring of 1984. The NCB and the government chose this moment to launch their provocation. At the beginning of March, the NCB announced plans for the closure of five pits in different areas of the coalfield. On Sunday 4 March, the 600 miners at Cortonwood in South Yorkshire, one of the threatened pits, voted to strike. The following day the Yorkshire NUM area council announced strike action of its 58,000 members from the last shift on Friday 9 March. With the threat of closure hanging over Polmaise colliery, the Scottish area council followed suit.

On 6 March, MacGregor announced the closure of 20 pits on "economic" grounds, with a loss of 20,000 jobs, knowing full well that it was the policy of the NUM only to accept the closure of pits on grounds of exhaustion. Scargill made it clear that NCB documents he had received showed that the plan was to close at least 70 pits with the loss of 70,000 jobs over a three-year period.

The NUM executive voted 21-3 to give official support to miners in Yorkshire and Scotland and any other areas that joined them. Area councils in Durham, Kent and South Wales called their members out from Monday, 12 March, and later in the month the Northumberland, Lancashire and North Derbyshire areas joined in. Already by 13 March, thousands of pickets were defying a High Court injunction taken out by the NCB banning them from crossing into Nottinghamshire to persuade the miners in the second largest coalfield in Britain to join the strike. The injunction, so easily brushed aside by the miners, was not pursued by the NCB for fear of provoking sympathy action by other unions. Both sides identified the Notts coalfield with its 30 pits, as one of the keys to the outcome of the strike. No effort or expense was spared by the NCB and the government in the campaign to keep the Notts miners from joining the strike.

The government implemented a rapid series of measures, prepared in advance, to prevent pickets getting into Notts. Thousands of extra police were drafted into the county from 16 separate forces, including the Met. A national police operation directed from Scotland Yard under the control of the Association of Chief Police Officers (ACPO) now swung into action. Roadblocks were set up around the county of Nottinghamshire. Kent miners found they could not get out of the county and were turned back at the Dartford Tunnel. Scottish miners were prevented from crossing the border into England. A High Court judge took only minutes to throw out the Kent NUM's demand for freedom of movement, and within two weeks of the start of the strike, the rough outlines of the form that the dispute would take were established.

The police, under the direction of the revived National Reporting Centre at Scotland Yard, were used to prevent flying pickets from gaining access to the working pits, and then as a battering ram against those miners – many of whom had walked across open country – that did make it. The police were ordered to begin mass arrests and to break the miners physically. Pickets' cars from Yorkshire were smashed with crowbars at illegal roadblocks. In his novel *GB84*, David Peace has one of his characters, a miner called Peter, describe being turned back from Notts:

> It was early when we got to pit. Load of coppers, though ...
> Fucking Met. Scum. Bloody lot of them. Arrogant scum and all
> – Do this. Do that. Don't do this. Don't do that ... Big Knob
> drove up to where we were stood around in cowfield. Got his

notebook out ready. Head darting about like a bloody pigeon. Right, he said to us. Where are you men from? I told him. I said, We're from Yorkshire. Are you indeed? he said. Indeed we are, I said. Right then, he said. Get back in your vehicles and fuck off back to Yorkshire. I said, That's not very nice language, Inspector. No, he said, and if you don't move, you'll hear more of it in Lincoln jail...

As attitudes hardened in the coalfields, the NCB and the government latched on to their central strategy for the strike: keep the NUM divided and organise the strike-breakers. "If we could keep Nottingham going," MacGregor wrote in his book *The Enemies Within: The story of the Miners Strike 1984-5*, "we could keep the lights on in Britain ... it was a tightrope exercise, for the men were by no means united or totally convinced from the outset that the strike was necessarily wrong."

On 15 March David Gareth Jones became the NUM's first martyr of the strike when he was killed by a flying brick at a mass picket of Ollerton Colliery in Notts. His family have remained bitter about the cursory nature of the investigation into his death. No serious attempt was made by the police to find out who threw the brick. "If it had been a policeman," his father Mark Jones wrote in his moving book *The Story of David Gareth Jones by his Father*, "they would have found out everything. They even found a woman who threw an egg at a lorry in Wales because she was a picket's wife, but they couldn't find out who threw a brick and killed my son." Five thousand miners from all over the country attended the emotional funeral in South Kirkby. Later in the strike Mark and Doreen Jones, David's parents, tore up a cheque for £250 sent by the scabs in Notts.

On March 29 the rail, sea and transport unions agreed to instruct their members to halt the movement of coal and coke, but the steel workers' union, led by the right-winger Bill Sirs, condemned this action and refused to allow a cut in steel production. A propaganda campaign was set in motion to encourage the demand for a ballot – which would of course have taken the steam out of the strike movement. This strategy of dividing the NUM, of driving a wedge between the so-called working miners and the majority, was carefully nurtured and developed by the NCB, the government, the police and the press over the course of the entire strike, with the purpose of discrediting it. The press, by and large, portrayed the miners as "violent thugs" for doing what miners and other trades unionists have always done – insisting on unity in the face of the enemy and no breaking of ranks.

The ballot red herring

The second month of the strike saw the demand for a ballot well and truly squashed. In the marches and rallies that ran alongside the daily mass pickets, one slogan was repeatedly voiced: "No Ballot". No-one in a pit with recent investment should have the right to vote another man out of work, those on strike insisted. The Notts men, in other words, whose pits tended to be more modern and produce more coal, and who even had separate incentive schemes, should not defy the unity of the strike.

To have halted the action or interrupted it in order to hold a time-consuming ballot, would have surrendered the initiative and the momentum of the strike to the government and its agents. There was little real substance in the argument for a ballot. Anti-union laws required the ballot as a condition for calling a strike precisely because it was seen by the Tories as a device for delaying, cooling down and dividing workers. But the ballot became the one demand continuously put to the NUM by the TUC trade union bureaucracy (whose policy was, actually, to defy the legislation) in order to hide their own lack of action, as a means of weakening the strike. The call for a ballot clearly was a red herring.

On the 25th anniversary of the start of the strike, Scargill wrote in *The Guardian* (7 March 2009):

> A question that has been raised time and time again over the past 25 years is: why did the union not hold a national strike ballot? Those who attack our struggle by vilifying me usually say: "Scargill rejected calls for a ballot."
> The real reason that NUM areas such as Nottinghamshire, South Derbyshire and Leicestershire wanted a national strike ballot was that they wanted the strike called off, believing naively that their pits were safe. Three years earlier, in 1981, there had been

no ballot when miners' unofficial strike action - involving Notts miners - had caused Thatcher to retreat from mass closures.

Scargill added:

> However, NUM areas had a right to ask the NEC to convene a special national delegate conference (as we had when calling the overtime ban) to determine whether delegates mandated by their areas should vote for a national individual ballot or reaffirm the decision of the NEC to permit areas such as Scotland, Yorkshire, South Wales and Kent to take strike action in accordance with Rule 41.
>
> Our special conference was held on 19 April. McGahey, Heathfield and I [the three NUM national officials] were aware from feedback that a slight majority of areas favoured the demand for a national strike ballot; therefore, we were expecting and had prepared for that course of action with posters, ballot papers and leaflets. A major campaign was ready to go for a "Yes" vote in a national strike ballot.
>
> At the conference, Heathfield told delegates in his opening address: "I hope that we are sincere and honest enough to recognise that a ballot should not be used and exercised as a veto to prevent people in other areas defending their jobs." His succinct reminder of the situation we were in opened up an emotional debate to which speaker after speaker made passionate and fiercely argued contributions.

The delegate conference, to the surprise of the miners' leaders, and to the elation of the 6,000 miners lobbying the meeting in Sheffield, rejected calls for a strike ballot, instead calling for miners not to cross picket lines and to extend the action. The question has to be asked: what would a national ballot have achieved? By all accounts the vote would have been close, and if it had come out in favour of the strike, most of the miners in Notts would probably have carried on working anyway.

The heavy daily confrontations between pickets and police in Notts and other areas escalated in Durham on 9 April when hundreds of miners surrounded the police station demanding the release of arrested pickets. On the same day over 80 pickets were arrested at the Babbington and Cresswell collieries in Notts. Another of Peace's miners in *GB84*, Martin, describes one of the mass pickets:

> Nowhere for us to go. Nowhere for us to run. Nowhere to hide – two lots of their riot squad coming out of woods. Each side of road. Trap us in a pincer movement or what-have-you – banging on their shields. Their dogs bloody barking – frightening. Fucking frightening – Nowhere to go. Nowhere but down ... No more arrests. Just assaults – Duffel coats. Anoraks. Parkas. Hats and scarves. Wellington boots. Docs. Ordinary boots and shoes. That's all we have – Nothing that can save us. That can save us from them – Lad behind me goes down. Down hard – perspex shield in back of neck. Truncheon on crown of head. Hear his skull crack. Hear him moan...

In all, over the year of the strike nearly 10,000 miners were arrested, and 8,000 of them charged. About 100 were jailed, including seven from the small coalfield in Kent who received brutal sentences of three and four years each. Around 1,700 were sacked for a variety of reasons. In the daily push and shove between miners and police at the entrance to the pits, many of the pickets were singled out and "snatched" by squads of police. The police mounted raids in the pubs where strikers were drinking and at the homes of supporters of the strike in Notts where the

Yorkshire pickets would stay overnight. Later in the strike, the police even arrested miners who tried to make a few pounds by "riddling" coal from the spoil tips and selling the bags and charged them with theft. In Grimethorpe in October the local community – men, women and children – stormed the police station after 22 miners were arrested for collecting coal on the tips.

The battle of Orgreave

The largest and most violent confrontations took place at the Orgreave Coke plant near Sheffield in May and June. Up to 10,000 miners and a similar number of police in para-military gear confronted each other on the fields above the plant in scenes that resembled a medieval battleground. Police repeatedly charged the miners on horseback with truncheons drawn. Dogs were also used. About 100 miners were arrested in the first big Battle of Orgreave in May, but scores more were assaulted. Scargill, who was observing the battle, was arrested. At the even larger Second Battle of Orgreave, on 18 June, many more were injured including Scargill who was struck by a riot shield. Of the Orgreave violence, Scargill said: "There have been scenes of almost unbelievable brutality... reminiscent of a Latin American police state."

The NUM had adapted the tactic of the mass picket from the 1972 miners' strike when thousands of engineers from Birmingham joined miners in closing a coke depot at Saltley Gate in Birmingham. This was the turning point of the 1972 dispute. But at Orgreave a similar approach failed. The coke plant was isolated in fields away from any other Sheffield factories. Although the miners closed down operations for a few hours, the plant quickly re-opened as the confrontation subsided and the convoys of coke to the Scunthorpe steelworks were resumed. The

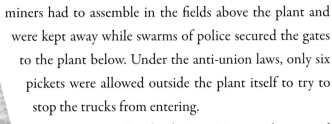

miners had to assemble in the fields above the plant and were kept away while swarms of police secured the gates to the plant below. Under the anti-union laws, only six pickets were allowed outside the plant itself to try to stop the trucks from entering.

In Scotland in May, police used increasingly violent tactics to ensure that convoys of scab coal reached the Ravenscraig steelworks. Sixty-five men were seized in one day on 7 May. The police numbered and photographed each striker as he was led away. These state attacks stirred up forces in the mining communities that had not been seen in earlier disputes – the women of the coalfields. In the first month of the strike, women from Kent and Yorkshire spearheaded the attempt to picket out the miners in Leicestershire. On 12 May, 10,000 miners' wives marched through Barnsley in the first national women's rally of the strike. The formation of the women's support groups all over the coalfields was a vital factor in stiffening the resistance of the miners to the closure programme. They were present in force at the huge rally of 45,000 in Mansfield, Nottinghamshire, on 14 May, called to answer a march of 5,000 strike-breakers in the town the previous week.

The women joined the strike effort at all levels: on the picket lines, in the soup kitchens which provided a meal a day to all in the community who needed it, as roving ambassadors of the strike, collecting money and drumming up support all over the country. At the end of 1984 they organised a joyful Christmas for the children of the coalfields in spite of the severe deprivations the communities were suffering. For many of them, this brought a change of outlook in their lives that has not been lost in the years since the strike ended. All of the pits had their own branches of Women Against Pit Closures and/or Women's Support Groups and many of them are still active today, 25 years on.

The Archive Awareness Campaign writes of the WAPC branches that they were a "support network composed of women who were all enduring the same hardships. This gave women a supportive environment in which to break away from traditional roles and develop and use new skills. It truly was a revolutionary experience for these women, who had previously led the sheltered life of wife and mother, to find they had skills, talents and strength that had previously been hidden".

Brenda Proctor, chair of the National WAPC told the *Guardian* (7 March 2009):

> We always said as women we lost nothing in the strike because we gained such a lot. We learned so much from it in terms of confidence and inspiration. Lots of women thought, 'if I can get up and talk to thousands of people at public meetings I can go on to other things', and went on to join councils or political groups. We learned politically from the disputes and went on to other strikes, like Wapping. We are still active and campaigning. It gave me confidence to go to college and then to university, where I took a degree in industrial relations, which wouldn't have happened if it hadn't been for the strike. I look back on it as the time of my life.

Supporters of the strike up and down the country were forced to find ways of giving help as individuals because of the TUC's inaction. Active support groups were set up in most areas to collect money, food, toys – anything that could be of use. These groups hosted visits by miners to address meetings of trade unionists and carry out street collections. They organised holidays and days out for the coalfield children. Hundreds of thousands of supporters of the strike got involved in these actions. By the end of October, after the seizure of all the NUM's assets by the courts, these support groups provided a vital lifeline for the running of the union. With the NUM accounts all frozen, the leaders had to rely on donations, large and small, just to keep the union functioning from day to day.

The strike attracted international support as no other dispute in Western Europe since the Second World War had done. The CGT union in France, in particular, rallied to the cause with large donations and two convoys of 40 lorries full of food and toys. They had to adopt extraordinary measures to get all this through the customs, but they found a way. There were contributions from Germany, Bulgaria, Hungary and many other countries. In April, Australian dockers and seamen refused to load a ship with 130,000 tons of coal and the blockade lasted the whole year of the strike. The Soviet Union stopped exporting coal to Britain, and there were many similar acts of solidarity throughout the world. The Tory government had, however, foreseen some of these actions and had spared no effort in finding alternative suppliers, of both oil and coal. In particular, the Stalinist regime of Poland proved ready and willing to increase its exports of coal. The NUM leaders lobbied the embassy furiously, but the coal continued coming. In September Polish officials announced an agreement to limit coal exports to Britain to 705,000 tons for the year. This was a transparent lie, as long before the deal was signed, by August in fact, over 900,000 tons had already been shipped to the UK.

Throughout the summer months of 1984, it became clear that the government was doing its utmost to starve the miners back to work by isolating them, by agreeing big pay increases to railway workers and others and through withholding social security payments to the strikers' families. But the government was relying ever more heavily on the TUC to withhold any meaningful support to the miners. The outcome of the strike remained in the balance. Big demonstrations of support were held regularly all

over the country, including one of 50,000 at the end of June in London when print workers came out in solidarity. The *Sun*, the *Mirror* and other papers did not appear the next day. Scargill told a meeting of trade unionists in July outside Saltley Gate in Birmingham, the scene of the famous mass picket of 1972: "We don't want pious words from leaders in the TUC ...We want industrial action in support of our union."

Also in July, Thatcher made her infamous speech: "We had to fight the enemy without in the Falklands. Now we are fighting the enemy within. It is more difficult to fight, but just as dangerous to liberty." Norman Tebbitt, minister for Trade and Industry, meanwhile denounced the NUM leaders as a "bunch of the most ruthless and violent bullies". Another picket, 55-year-old Joe Green, a friend of Scargill, was crushed to death by a lorry outside Ferrybridge power station, South Yorkshire. More than 8,000 miners, led by a Scottish piper, joined the procession through Pontefract to the crematorium. Miners at two pits in Kent and one in North Derbyshire occupied their places of work and were sacked. Violence flared inside Yorkshire, as the NCB in a blatant provocation encouraged a few lone strike-breakers to return to work. Barricades were erected at Rossington on 9 July, while later the same day police ran amok in Fitzwilliam, storming into a pub, terrorising customers and beating up miners and their wives. This was class war as never seen before in Britain.

The government, meanwhile, felt confident enough in the treacherous role of the TUC to step up the pursuit of the NUM in the courts. At the beginning of August, 2,500 miners from all over the country turned up in Pontypridd to keep the sequestrators away after a High Court judge had threatened the assets of the South Wales NUM. The Welsh NUM refused to pay a £50,000 fine for contempt so the judge issued an order grabbing £707,000 of the union's funds. At the end of August the NCB had found another lone scab to break the strike at Gascoigne Wood in the Selby coalfield. The police baton-charged a huge picket of 6,000 miners to smuggle him into the pit. Squads of riot police invaded the pit communities of Hatfied and Armthorpe the following week. In London, a huge demonstration of 20,000 women, many of them marching for the first time, filed through the capital and listened as Scargill again demanded industrial action from the TUC.

The NCB tactic of finding the odd individual to break the strike in Yorkshire was all of a piece with the general state of lawlessness and violence provoked by the police in the coalfields.

Peter, in *GB84*, describes the scabs:

> Poor blokes on these buses. Their startled faces behind wire cages welded to windows – Drivers with crash helmets. Pigs on back seat. Them sat on aisle side – but I knew them faces. Everybody did – Every pit had faces like theirs. Faces with little eyes that never met yours. Eyes that'd sooner stare at their boots or ground. Faces of a certain type, they were. Type that hated their work. Type that were out sick more often than not. Type that never pulled their weight. Type that always wanted union to do this, that and other for them. Cowed and broken men before strike even began. Shirkers or gaffers' narks. Area managers and chief constables had leaned on them hard. Broken them in two all over again – it wasn't pit managers' bloody idea. Pit managers knew them too well – knew them of old. Knew what they were worth – Nothing. Fuck all. Just like this scab they'd got going in here at Silverwood. He'd have been fucking sacked years ago if it wasn't for us...

Although fictional, this is a fair representation of what the miners thought of these heroes of the Tory tabloid press.

TUC offers words but no action

The spectre of the strike, picking up momentum and heat through the summer, came to dominate proceedings at both the TUC Congress in September and the Labour Party conference in October. TUC delegates gave Scargill a standing ovation. Miners from Cortonwood, who had marched all the way from Yorkshire to Brighton, lobbied Congress and demanded a General Strike. A string of union leaders, including right-wingers David Basnett (who was later to attack "Scargillism") and Gavin Laird (who talked of power cuts within weeks) mounted the rostrum to declare they would never allow the NUM to be broken by the Tories. Nearly all of them also pledged their backing for a ban on the movement of coal, coke and oil.

But behind the scenes, TUC heavyweights had insisted on wording the motion so that decisions would only be implemented after detailed discussions between the TUC General Council and the affected unions. The power supply workers, the steelworkers and the electricians all voted against the motion.

MacGregor in his book says the trade union movement in general "found itself talking more and more about the need to support the miners, but doing less and less to help Scargill". He elaborates later in the book: "There was very little they [the trade union leaders] were willing to do to help his struggle, but in order to keep up the front of brotherly comradeship, they found themselves constrained to offer a lot of verbal support." He thought the TUC wanted "to find a way of making sure Scargill is beaten without the miners losing". At the Labour Party conference, delegates voted to condemn police violence and gave full support to the strike, but party leader Kinnock used the opportunity to blame the miners for violence and referred to the police as "meat in the sandwich".

Almost unbelievably, Scargill was served with a writ for contempt of court inside the conference itself. This arose from one of the many attempts of government and NCB-inspired strike-breakers to tie the union up in legal proceedings. This particular attempt was set in train by two Yorkshire scabs, but behind the initiative were the NCB and a sinister individual called David Hart, an old Etonian and an anti-socialist zealot who had the ear of both Thatcher and MacGregor. Hart travelled round the coalfields in a chauffeur-driven limousine setting up a network of strike-breakers under the auspices of the "National Working Miners Committee".

He became a kind of freelance organiser of strike-breakers. According to *Guardian* journalist Seamus Milne in his book *The Enemy within: MI5, Maxwell and the Scargill Affair*, in the autumn of 1984 Hart reported to Thatcher directly by phone and became the coal board chairman's closest adviser. Later in the strike, he was, writes Milne, "intimately involved in the frantic efforts to prevent the pit deputies from joining the NUM strike". He also warned Thatcher that any negotiated settlement with the NUM would be politically undesirable. "It was essential, Hart believed, that the miners should be forced to return to work without a settlement," Milne writes. Hart, "according to highly placed police and Whitehall sources", also maintained close links with Stella Rimington, the director-general of MI5 who co-ordinated the agency's operations against the miners, as he roamed the country plotting and organising strikebreakers.

25

MacGregor refers to Hart as his "Indian Scout" in Nottinghamshire. Hart, he wrote, assisted the working miners "in launching campaigns to go after the NUM on legal grounds". He describes in his book the importance the NCB attached to the campaign to identify potential strike-breakers in all the coalfields, but particularly, as the strike wore on, in Yorkshire. He also spelled out why he avoided initiating any legal action from the NCB directly or using the government's anti-union laws. Any such action would tend to unite all the unions behind the NUM, he thought.

In September 1984, the High Court ruled the strike unofficial and unlawful. Scargill, unsurprisingly, rejected the High Court ruling, declaring: "There is no High Court judge going to take away the democratic right of our union to deal with its own internal affairs." His stance was supported by the NUM national executive and a special delegates' conference. Solicitors then applied for leave to bring contempt proceedings. The order was issued. Hart chartered a helicopter, flew to London to collect the writ server, landed in Blackpool and then organised a phony press pass to sneak the official into the conference hall, where he served the writ on the outraged NUM president in front of a *Daily Express* photographer. A second writ was served on Scargill on October 5 for simply declaring in public that the strike was official.

The following week the union was fined £200,000 and Scargill £1,000 for contempt. The NUM ignored the fines in line with TUC official policy, although an anonymous donor paid Scargill's. On 25 October, the High Court ordered the sequestration of the union's entire assets. The following month a receiver was appointed and for 18 months all the NUM's money and property were in the hands of this court-appointed official receiver. The union had been expecting sequestration and had taken precautions by instructing the NUM chief executive Roger Windsor to move the money to untraceable accounts all over Europe. In the event, the money was speedily tracked down. The strike organisers from now on were forced to live from hand to mouth, paying the costs of the union and the strike in cash.

October and November were the months when, as Thatcher herself later admitted, the government nearly lost the strike. Had the leaders of the labour movement been only half-committed to a miners' victory, this was a moment of real opportunity. The government was finding it more and more difficult to hold the line, and was very nervous of the prospect of support for the miners from other groups of workers. As early as July, Thatcher and her cabinet had faced one such emergency, when dockers went on strike over the unloading of a coal boat at Immingham by non-registered labour. Within days the strike had developed into a national dispute, bringing all the docks to a standstill. The government was even preparing to bring in troops, as lorries were backed up on the motorways to Dover and other ports. But after assurances guaranteeing the integrity of the National Dock Labour Scheme, the dockers were sent back to work by TGWU leaders.

In September, a second dock strike broke out when a giant iron ore ship, the *Ostia*, docked at Hunterston, near the Ravenscraig steelworks in Scotland. She was unloaded by steel workers after dockers had refused to touch her. A national strike followed, but again transport union leaders and the Scottish TUC cobbled together a shabby deal whereby the supply of scab coal to Ravenscraig was actually increased. The NUM immediately rejected the sell-out deal, and continued picketing the port at Hunterston. The government, once again, had survived, not at all through its own initiatives but through the cowardly behaviour of the union leaders.

27

Nacods are bought off

The greatest concern in the government revolved around the actions of Nacods, the union of the colliery deputies or under-managers who had responsibility for the safety of the pits. It was crucial that this union should not throw in its lot with the NUM as this could have closed the Nottinghamshire coalfield. The attitude of MacGregor was a bit different. He thought that even if Nacods pursued the strike option, their members in Notts could and would be persuaded to continue working, thus keeping the coalfield open. At the end of September, Nacods members voted by 82.5% for an all-out strike, and seemed to agree with the NUM that pits could not be closed solely on economic grounds if there was still coal to be mined. The government panicked. Energy Minister Peter Walker told Macgregor that "you must be out of your mind" to risk a confrontation with Nacods. Downing Street summoned him to see the Prime Minister and (according to MacGregor) was told by Thatcher: "Well, I'm very worried about it. You have to realise that the fate of this government is in your hands, Mr. MacGregor. You have got to solve this problem."

The Nacods' leadership set 26 October as the date for its 15,000 members to begin their strike. The decision was never implemented, however. Two days before the strike was due to begin, a backstage deal was done. The union accepted an unprincipled compromise whereby the NCB would review the closure programme. Nacods were promised an "independent" review of all proposed pit closures before they were implemented. But the review process would only have an advisory status and was essentially meaningless.

According to Milne, Thatcher said she remained "unclear" why the deputies had settled and saved her skin. Scargill too remains mystified. In his *Guardian* article of 7 March 2009, he homes in on this "inexplicable decision" by Nacods, describing it as a disaster. The NUM and Nacods had worked out a common programme to resist pit closures, he says. "Nacods members had recorded an 82% ballot vote for strike action, and their leaders made it clear to the NCB that unless the Nacods-NUM terms were accepted the Nacods strike would go ahead. I was later told by a Tory who had been a minister at the time that when Thatcher was informed of the Nacods-NUM agreement she announced to the cabinet 'special committee' that the government had no choice but to settle the strike on the unions' terms."

When she learned that Nacods had called off its strike and accepted a "modified" colliery review procedure, Thatcher withdrew the government's decision to settle,

Scargill says. "The monumental betrayal by Nacods has never been explained in a way that makes sense. Even the TUC recognised that the Nacods settlement was a disaster. The fact that Nacods' leaders ignored pleas from the NUM and TUC not to call off their strike or resile [draw back] from their agreement with the NUM not only adds mystery but poses the question – whose hand did the moving, and why?"

Pressure was building in other areas too. In November, the government had to deal with serious strikes in the car industry. High Court writs were issued against nine of the unions as a strike at British Leyland's Austin Rover plants began. The following day, the courts ordered six of them to call off their action for failing to hold a ballot under the Tory anti-union laws. Later in the month the TGWU was fined £200,000 for refusing to call off official action at Austin Rover. The High Court also ordered Cardiff dockers to call off their boycott action against two strike-breaking haulage firms. And on 22 November, the state pressed home its attack when the House of Lords rejected an appeal by civil service unions against the abolition of trade union rights at GCHQ Cheltenham.

At the same time, a number of Labour councils, led by Lambeth and Liverpool, were engaged in a massive popular resistance to Tory spending cuts. They organised demonstrations and rallies and were threatening to refuse to set a rate that would in practice devastate local services. Like the miners, however, they received no support from Labour's national leaders. It was also in November that Paul Holmes, 15, and his brother Darren, 14, from Goldthorpe, Yorkshire, were killed while digging for coal on a railway embankment.

Yet, despite the mounting resistance to the Tories, the TUC and Labour Party leaders point blank refused to act. Miners and their wives at a rally in Aberavon, South Wales, booed and jeered Norman Willis in his first speech as the new general secretary of the TUC as he criticised strikers for their actions, saying: "For I have to say that any miner, too, who resorts to violence, wounds the miners' case far more than they damage their opponents' resolve. Violence creates more violence …" Slow-handclapping gave way to loud cheers as an impromptu noose was lowered in front of Willis who broke off his speech and sat down. The Tory press praised his speech. The following day Kinnock told Welsh miners that his diary was too full to join them on the picket line to witness police tactics, the same excuse that he made earlier in the month for not making himself available at a series of rallies called by the NUM with the aim of broadening the dispute.

At a rally in Derby, Scargill appealed once more to other union members: "We need you to take industrial action to stop the flow of coal and oil and abide by the TUC guidelines adopted in September at the Congress." Some have accused Scargill of deliberately keeping the TUC on the sidelines out of the struggle because of their role in the 1926 general strike and lock-out of miners. In fact, from June, Scargill had insistently called for support from the TUC. Unbelievably, it was not until November, eight months into the strike, that the TUC finally set up a hardship fund, which miners tended to see as a sop to excuse its refusal to organise industrial action.

By December, deprived of their funds, the union had to rely on cash collections from miners' support groups that sprung up in every town and city to survive and prosecute the strike. It was at this vulnerable time that a group of Communist Party members on the NUM executive joined forces with the right wing of the union in an attempt to force the delegates to vote for the return of the miners' funds to Britain, where they would have been immediately seized. This attempt to appease the courts was rejected, much to the discomfiture of the Scottish Stalinists. The delegates also backed a resolution calling on the TUC to hold a Special General Council meeting to "mobilise industrial action to stop this most vicious threat in our history".

Kinnock denounced all talk of a General Strike soon after and the TUC refused to recall the General Council, preferring instead to make an appeal directly to Downing Street. Scargill was obliged to remark: "We don't want the TUC or anyone else to go along and argue a case that effectively undermines the arguments of the NUM. We want the decisions of the TUC conference in September put into practical effect." A 24-hour picket was mounted over the Christmas period at every pit in the country, and the women organised a dinner, toys and a party for all children.

In January 1985, sterling began to plummet on the money markets, as speculators realised that Thatcher may have mis-calculated over the miners' resistance. The pound sank at one stage to below 1.05 to the dollar, a big blow to government plans as all the extra imported oil had to be paid for in dollars.

Also in January the Midland Bank had to be rescued by the Bank of England with a £2bn injection of taxpayers' money. The strike was still largely solid, though from the NCB propaganda, dutifully reported by the press, an impartial observer would have imagined that the strike was collapsing. Talks set up by Peter Heathfield with the NCB for 21 January 1985 were once again sabotaged by the government. Thatcher decreed that the NUM had to give a written undertaking to accept the closure of pits on economic grounds before talks could begin. The *Morning Star* of 25 January poisonously suggested this condition was acceptable, but the NUM executive backed Scargill in his refusal to accept it.

The TUC leaders were acutely aware of the growing support for the demand of a General Strike as the only way of achieving the miners' demands and of avoiding a humiliating defeat for the whole working class. This kind of perspective, involving a struggle for power in Britain filled them with horror. The TUC itself relied on the whole-hearted assistance of the Stalinists of the Communist Party, whose position was based on their own opposition to the General Strike. The *Morning Star* at this point floated the idea of a return to work without a settlement, but "with heads held high". The Communist Party was in the process of splitting into two, but both wings were hostile to the idea of a general strike; the *Morning Star* group was the mouthpiece of the trade union bureaucracy, whose control of the unions would have been lost in the event of a General Strike, while the Eurocommunist wing was increasingly hostile to the uncompromising stance of the NUM leaders and was closer to Kinnock.

It was a manifestation of the weakness of the Thatcher government that its dependence on the TUC, who were patently not going to support the miners in any significant way, became greater as the strike developed. The government agreed to secret meetings between Willis and MacGregor and even left it to Willis to present the NCB's "final offer" to the NUM executive. The executive was summoned to London by Willis, but rejected the offer. On 18 February the TUC leaders announced they were to visit Thatcher. Scargill said the NUM was not a party to the talks. Willis submitted a second document to the executive and told them it was the best they could get. Angry NUM executive members declared that the document was 100% worse than the first one. The delegates rejected it unanimously the next day. On 24 February, 50 weeks after the start of

31

the strike, the miners and their supporters still managed to rally 30,000 people in London.

On 3 March, however, a return-to-work resolution was narrowly passed at an NUM delegate conference. Yorkshire, Scotland and Kent voted against going back without the reinstatement of sacked miners, but the vote for a return was 98-91 in favour. The idea for a united organised end to the strike without a settlement had been pushed by Kim Howells, a leading Eurocommunist and a full-time employee of the NUM at the time, and now a loyal New Labour MP. "The move," according to Milne, "which had been secretly planned by a small group in South Wales and backed by Kinnock and the CPGB's Euro communist wing, created a snowball effect and rapidly led to the narrow conference vote to call off the stoppage".

Scargill, who had favoured a continuation of the strike, said after the decision to end the strike: "This union's position has been maintained and the credibility, not only of the leadership, but of those tremendous men and women who have suffered for 12 months, has also been maintained. I believe that the fact that this union has struggled for 12 months is itself a magnificent achievement."

Civil war in Hatfield

An eye-witness account by Ray Rising, a *News Line* photographer during the 1984-5 strike.

Stainforth, near Doncaster in South Yorkshire, and its adjacent coal mine of Hatfield Main, was witness to some extraordinary sights one sultry day in August 1984. They testified to the civil war nature of the miners' strike.

The strike had been going for five months and not a single strike-breaker had dared to challenge the village by attempting to go to work. But on 21 August all that changed. Three scabs, we were told, had broken the strike and had gone in soon after dawn to the accompaniment of many flying missiles and protection from the Greater Manchester Constabulary.

Reporter Simon Vevers and myself had been at Armthorpe, three miles away, when a message from one of Simon's innumerable contacts in the area was passed to us about the earlier "goings on" at Hatfield Main. We hightailed down there to find not a stand-off but a sit-off.

A detachment from London's Met, meanwhile, had reinforced police lines whilst the whole village, including older men, women and children, were behind miners who were sat across the end of the pit lane in a blockade. The time was approaching when the police would bring out the vehicle containing the scabs through the only exit from the pit.

The strike-breakers hadn't gotten their hands dirty for pay that day. Their purpose was purely to create a psychological wedge in the village and facilitate the use of the big city forces mobilised to do their worst. There were no token attempts at negotiation with the miners and villagers on the part of senior police officers. They knew why they were there.

It mattered not to them that one of the scabs had been gently persuaded to rejoin the strike and had left the ferrying wagon, with now just two aboard, for the gauntlet run through Stainforth's defiant lines.

The mercury was rising and we could sense the fidgety impatience throughout the ranks of the closely packed, overdressed lines of blue. On a simple signal both left and right wings of police charged forward, punching, kicking and truncheoning all before them. Of course, the majority of the miners climbed to their feet and scattered to avoid the blows.

Others held their ground and were overwhelmed with hardwood sticks, steel toe-capped boots and shields. Men, women and children ran. There were subsequently many days like this at Stainforth with divisions of police horses and dog-handlers rampaging through the little alleyways that criss-crossed the miners' housing.

Some months later I was asked to print four sets of photos for a forthcoming court case in Doncaster. A miner who had been collared immediately the police charge had started was now, we learned, being charged with assaulting the police! The fact that he had stopped breathing after his beating and had been resuscitated in the emergency room did not alter the fact of his victimisation.

The pictures clearly showed his distinctive T-shirt being enveloped by a sea of blue. He obviously had neither time nor weapons for any assault against the police. On the day in court, the files of photographs were passed to the solitary circuit judge, prosecution counsel, defence counsel and myself.

After affirming to tell the truth, the prosecution questioned me, not on what I had seen as a witness, but as to whether my exhibits could be trusted – being that I worked for a revolutionary newspaper! The judge interjected, countering the prosecutor with, "the witness is here to confirm the validity of the photographs – do you question their truth?" The police prosecutor bowed his head and said, "No your honour."

Had the prosecution embarrassed the judge with their witch-hunt of objective truth? No matter, the judge duly found the miner guilty on the verbal from several of Manchester's law enforcers. Photo evidence was obviously inferior to police testimony. He got three months.

These court cases were repeated with monotonous and banging-up regularity over the ensuing months of the strike and well after it had ended. Justice is class justice, always was, always will be - better be the day when the "rules of court" and judgements are passed down by the working class themselves.

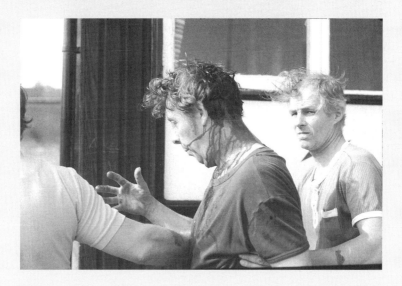

2

Return to work

THE STRIKE SHOWED that given a leadership that told the truth and fought on principles, workers would fight heroically and tenaciously for their jobs and rights. And the year-long campaign also demonstrated the reverse – a leadership that is tied to the status quo can never challenge the system of which it is a vital part. Labour Party leaders even dispensed with the pretence of supporting the miners, so concerned were they to keep their hands and noses clean to prove their calibre as responsible politicians of the capitalist system.

The mis-named Communist Party which wielded a great deal of influence in the NUM, with members on the executive and amongst the delegates, was also exposed in the course of the strike. All sections of the party remained wedded to Stalinism, which from the mid-1920s onwards had undermined and then broken the back of the Moscow-based communist movement. The party's commitment to the "parliamentary road to socialism" inevitably meant tail-ending and providing a cover for the Labour and trade union bureaucracies.

There was no criticism of the treacherous role of the TUC leaders, while the NCB and the Tory Party were portrayed as people who could be "brought to their senses". That was the sentiment behind the *Morning Star* headline a few weeks before the decision of the NUM delegates to return to work: "The basis for talks exists – force the NCB to the Table". In reality, there was no basis for talks as the strike was against the right of the NCB to close pits on economic grounds alone. The NCB had not changed its position on this and Thatcher herself had re-stated the condition for further talks – that the NUM had to accept the principle that the NCB could close pits on economic grounds alone. The *Morning Star* was merely seeking to advance the hopes of the trade union bureaucrats trying to call off this bitter struggle. The so-called Eurocommunist wing disgraced itself by scheming against the NUM leadership. The Euros from Maerdy pit in South Wales appeared on TV to plug the line of returning to work without an agreement and without the reinstatement of the sacked miners.

The Militant (now Socialist Party), true to form, did not understand the strike for what it really was: a challenge for power. An analysis by Ken Smith in 2004, *A Civil War Without Guns. 20 years on, the lessons of the 1984-5 miners' strike*, is essentially a reformist one. He sees the strike as being played out within the system rather than one that threatened to blow it apart and bring the government down. The revolutionary implications of the strike are never brought out. This is shown by the conclusion that if the miners had won, it would have resulted in "a huge sweeping movement to the left inside the workers' organisations and in society generally" and perhaps a Tory defeat at the subsequent election – and no more. The Militant/Socialist Party also retrospectively called for a ballot: "During the strike, Militant maintained a united stand with the miners and the NUM and argued against the hypocrisy of the right wing unions over the ballot ... But after the strike Militant maintained that, because of the way the issue was used in the movement to cut across the miners struggle, a ballot should have been called."

Apart from the Communist Party, the main influence on the course of the strike came from the Workers Revolutionary Party (WRP) and its daily newspaper, the *News Line*. From the start, the WRP understood the miners' strike as a challenge for power against the government, and saw the struggle for jobs and communities as incompatible with the plans of the Thatcher government, and even with capitalism itself. A WRP statement in April 1984 said: "The Bonapartist regime [Thatcher] is determined not to give way – which means the working class can only win through bringing down the government and smashing the capitalist state."

From June 1984, when it had become evident that the strike had become a political battle with the government, and that the government was using the forces of the state to smash the NUM, the WRP called for a General Strike in support of the miners. In a statement at the end of the strike, the WRP said: "The NUM's demand carried at the TUC in September that no union should cross an NUM picket line was a step in the direction of a General Strike. Implementation of this demand and the associated call for power workers not to handle scab coal would have provoked a government-employer lock-out, sequestration and fines – and with them a massive escalation of the class struggle to the point of a General Strike. Not accidentally, the TUC – having adopted the NUM demand – abandoned it immediately."

The leaders of the NUM stood firm and demanded support from the TUC. Workers were under attack in many industries and a General Strike would have united car workers, dockers, GCHQ workers (who had had their right to join a union taken away), bringing in the unemployed, local government workers and Labour councils that were defying the government. After the strike, the WRP organised a March to Free the Jailed Miners which culminated in a mass rally at Alexandra Palace in July 1985. The platform included Jack Collins, Kent NUM secretary, Notts NUM secretary Henry Richardson, Ann Lilburn, national chair of Women Against Pit Closures, Ted Knight, leader of the rate-capped Lambeth Council and Anne Scargill, wife of the NUM president. Immediately following the rally, a series of provocations led to the split and subsequent break-up of the WRP in which the state played a role.

Many miners resented the circumstances of the return to work. They felt they could have got a better deal and should not have gone back without an agreement to reinstate the sacked miners at least. According to Seumas Milne's book, Kim Howells' call for a return to work led to a "ferocious row" on the telephone with Scargill. Milne quotes Tyrone O'Sullivan, the area president of the South Wales miners: "Kim Howells ... was hated in the pits after the strike. He was an unelected officer and had no mandate to say we were going back to work." Howells, together with Kevin Barron, an MP who had remained loyal to the NUM through the strike, went on to serve a new kind of master. From their positions of political respectability alongside Neil Kinnock, they both played active roles in the ferocious witch-hunt of Scargill and Heathfield launched by Robert Maxwell's *Daily Mirror* in 1990, while Howells would become a New Labour minister.

After a year on strike, miners returned to work behind their banners and brass bands, "heads held high". But the industry was never the same again as pit managers imposed ruthless new work regimes and sacked many of the key strikers, egged on by a triumphant attitude on the part of MacGregor and the NCB. Redundancies and closures followed soon after. But the NUM did not accept the role of a defeated army allotted to it by the press and the government. At the NUM conference in 1985, a few months after the strike ended, Scargill told delegates: "The only way is to fight again with the same determination, the same pride."

The NCB, backed by the government, not only encouraged the breakaway scab union in Nottinghamshire, the Union of Democratic Miners (UDM), but actively conspired with its leaders to help it along every step of the way towards eventual recognition by the board. In the middle of this conspiracy was a certain Charlie Falconer, who had already played a role in the strike itself as one of the lawyers acting for the NCB in obtaining a High Court injunction to stop Yorkshire miners picketing the Notts pits. Francis Beckett and David Hencke in their book *Marching to the Faultline* reveal that Falconer's legal services and advice "played a crucial role in the creation of the Union of Democratic Miners (UDM) which was to become a running sore to the NUM for the rest of the century." Falconer was a close friend of Tony Blair and became Lord Chancellor in the Blair government of 1997.

The leaders of the NUM struggled to hold the line in almost impossible circumstances after the strike. After the seizure of the union's funds in October 1984, the NUM leaders had to resort to extraordinary measures to keep the union afloat. Special accounts were set up for money donated by other unions and supporters. Cash came pouring into the NUM offices in boxes and plastic-bags. It had to be processed, counted and recorded and it was this vital but, inevitably, chaotic process that exposed the union to allegations of fraud.

What also made the union vulnerable was the infighting and political differences that built up within the leadership of the union after the end of the strike. Serious opposition to Scargill's leadership coalesced around the Eurocommunist wing of the Communist Party – particularly strong in South Wales and Scotland – leading to the spectacle of these Stalinists making common cause with the right wing of the union against Scargill and Heathfield, the general secretary; Labour's leaders gave active support to this opposition. As the pit closure programme accelerated, the bitterness grew, and some NUM staff joined the "Get Scargill" fifth column.

Roger Windsor, the chief executive of the NUM from 1983-1989 and Jim Parker, Scargill's former driver approached the *Daily Mirror*, and sold their "stories" for cash. In March 1990, around the time the union was preparing to oppose a fresh closure programme, the *Daily Mirror*, owned by the corrupt fraudster Robert Maxwell, and ITV's the *Cook Report* simultaneously ran an "exposé", alleging that Scargill and Heathfield had diverted money donated to the union to pay off their mortgages – funds, moreover, which had come from Libya, a country considered to be beyond the pale by the government and the press. Scargill and Heathfield did not even have mortgages, but this did not stop the press frenzy. The "full and shocking truth", later exposed as a pack of lies, grew into a speculative free-for-all. An orchestrated series of allegations were invented about "missing" Russian money, dodgy bank accounts and even a request by Scargill for guns!

This witch-hunt deliberately targeted Scargill and Heathfield because they remained firm both during and after the strike. It destabilised the NUM on the eve of the announcement of another round of pit closures, which was undoubtedly one of its intentions. Thatcher always feared a second strike and the timing of the witch-hunt was surely not accidental. In *The Enemy within: MI5, Maxwell and the Scargill Affair*, Milne gives a full account of the sinister role of the secret services, the police Special Branch, MI5 and GCHQ, not only during the strike itself but as covert players in the Scargill affair of 1990. "At every stage and in every aspect of the affair [the witch-hunt], the fingerprints of the intelligence services could be found like an unmistakeable calling card." Of the strike itself, he writes that there was "unquestionably a deliberate and meticulously constructed attempt to set up the miners' leadership during the most finely balanced weeks of the dispute".

Milne concludes: "The use of informers, infiltrators and provocateurs; premeditated police violence; attempted frame-ups, bugging and surveillance on a heroic scale; the spending of billions of pounds on facing down the strike and then on forcing through large-scale pit closures; none of this commands any public

43

consensus ... Such an assault had nothing whatever to do with the defence of democracy. Indeed it represented the very opposite."

Heathfield told the union's annual conference in 1992: "I've aged 15 years in the last five ... Every agency of the state was directed against Arthur Scargill and myself ... and every allegation has been found groundless. I had no difficulty coming to terms with the attacks of the Maxwells and the tabloid media – my class awareness and the knowledge that it was a load of codswallop meant I was able to come to terms with that. But, I have to say to you comrades, I have not come to terms with being sued by colleagues on the national executive committee..."

In 1991, the NCB announced a new round of closures throughout the coalfields, including Notts. The NUM executive won a ballot for action against the closures and a huge demonstration seemed to suggest that the mood against the Tories and their blind support for the market economy was hardening. The government backed off for a while, but the crisis passed. The closure programme went ahead and the rump of the industry was privatised in 1993. Today there are only 19 working deep-mine pits in the country, many of them small. Most of the coal used in the power stations is imported at a cost of between £2 billion and £3 billion a year.

With pits closing, the communities around them were thrown into crisis. Drugs, thieving and anti-social behaviour all became big problems. The new jobs created in the mining areas were mostly low-paid. According to a study published in the *Financial Times* in March 2009, the number of adults claiming incapacity benefit in the English and Welsh coalfields was a staggering 336,000 in 2007. And since the financial crash in September 2008, the number of unemployed men claiming benefit has risen between 75-100% depending on the area. These regions are "ill-equipped to weather the recession", the report said. The stability of these former thriving communities in the coalfields including those in Notts, it would be fair to say, has been destroyed, with some of them turned into wastelands.

The end of the miners' strike signalled the start of a long slide towards the relative impotence of the trade unions under a leadership which had thrown in the towel. After the miners, the printers, sacked by Rupert Murdoch when he moved his printing operations from Fleet Street to Fortress Wapping in 1986, were condemned to the same fate: the sack, masked by the usual rhetoric from the TUC and the Labour Party leadership.

The way forward

THE MINERS' STRIKE BROUGHT HOME to many the class nature and the repressive role of the capitalist state. It also demonstrated with absolute clarity the impossibility of reforming the state, of changing its nature, through parliamentary debate or extra-parliamentary pressure. It was no real surprise that the trade union bureaucracy did not support the miners. Union leaders in Britain have alway shied away from any struggle against the state that poses the question of power. This is because the state provides the essential ideological, political, legal, educational and coercive framework for the functioning of capitalist society, which includes a role for union bureaucrats to police the working class.

Parliament itself decides almost nothing. Whatever limited powers it once possessed were long ago transferred to the executive in the shape of the prime minister, the cabinet and the institutions of the state itself. The creation, for example, of the national police force under the control of ACPO in 1984 that invaded Nottinghamshire and other mining areas, was not even referred to the

House of Commons. All those concerned about defeating global capitalism have to take forward the main lesson of the miners' strike: that it is plainly not possible to win a battle against the government and the state over jobs or other major questions without having a perspective of transforming how power operates in Britain. This is inseparable from developing policies and ideas that take us beyond the status quo.

The miners faced challenges which are now back on the social agenda 25 years later. Global capitalism has struck the buffers. The collapse of the financial system has precipitated a meltdown in the economy. Millions of jobs are on the line and neither the capitalist system nor the capitalist state has any answers outside of imposing the full weight of the crisis on the working class. The banks are on life support, barely breathing despite the billions pumped into the financial system. A slump deeper and more widespread than the 1930s looms. On top of all this, climate change, itself a consequence of the uncontrolled drive for profit under capitalism, is out of control and is a clear and immediate threat to the well-being of people and planet.

The economic crash is changing everyone's life. As tens of millions of workers all over the world lose their jobs, as savings and pensions disappear and as homes are re-possessed by the banks, more and more people will question the nature of a system that can only deliver poverty and homelessness for many, grotesque inequality, economic slump and war. None of the great problems facing humanity can be solved whilst global corporations compete for profit and nation states go to war on their behalf for resources and markets.

The political parties at Westminster all stand exposed as collaborators of this system, unable even to address, let alone solve any of the problems of the world. They are divided only in the detail of policy. All of them agree on the main task: to save the system at the expense of working people while protecting their own privileges. There will be no shortage of new forces to challenge capitalism, though these may not appear in the old form of powerful trade unions. What is equally certain is that, in this coming period, widespread social unrest and anger will be provoked by the attempts of government to keep the system on the rails. People are already looking for answers.

So if real changes can only be won today by challenging and defeating the state then policies have to be developed and put forward for this objective. The changes in the last 30 years in the way that capitalism operates have to be understood and grasped in order for there to be a conscious break with the old policies and formulas of the past. *Unmasking the State – a rough guide to real democracy*, by Paul Feldman and published by A World to Win, explains:

> Transformed by the march of global capitalism, the state is unable and unwilling in this period to uphold or sustain the democratic forms that have allowed it to rule over the majority. Without new democratic forms, it is inconceivable that we could reorganise the economy along not-for-profit lines, put an end to war and act on the ecological crisis. Without a comprehensive revolutionary regime change we cannot breathe new life into democratic achievements and make the right to vote mean something again. Representative democracy was a great step forward in the historic struggle for rights. It enabled working people to build independent political parties like the Labour Party and win significant reforms through the parliamentary process. But that period of history has drawn to a close with the emergence of the market state, marked in Britain by the transformation of Labour into capitalist New Labour.

"The 1984-5 strike," explains *Unmasking the State*, "marked the early period of corporate-driven globalisation, which has changed the way capitalism operates. State power is now more openly revealed as the political and ugly face of capitalism, both domestic and particularly transnational ... Despite the widespread assumption that capitalist democracy was once the only future worth talking about, the British state no longer has that allure." That the constitutional crisis provoked over MPs' expenses led to ordinary people talking about the "need for revolution" to clean up the political system confirms this analysis. As the book concludes:

> The existing parliamentary system is a façade that increasingly undermines and devalues the right to vote that was won in bitter struggle against the ruling classes. A single vote every four or

five years in a general election cannot alter the fact that this form of democracy is limited and curtailed in so many ways that reform is impossible. We should, instead, see the achievement of representative democracy as a stepping stone to greater things.

A World to Win is building a movement to struggle for the implementation of a People's Charter for Democracy, which calls for a constitution that would:

1. End the rule of political élites and bureaucracies and instead create new local, regional and national Assemblies, representing diverse communities and workplaces.
2. Extend democracy through co-operative forms of ownership and workplace control of major corporations, enterprises and services.
3. Establish social rights to housing, education, health, transport, training, employment, pensions and care in older age.
4. Guarantee basic human rights to organise, strike, speak and act free from state surveillance and interference.
5. Safeguard the civil and religious rights of minority communities and adopt a "no borders" approach to refugees and asylum seekers.
6. Eliminate speculation and profit as the basis for society, ensuring that both ecological care and basic human needs shape production, consumption and lifestyles.

"To this end", says the Charter, "we will work to establish local and national Conventions for Democracy to build support for the transfer of political and economic power to the majority." In other words, a revolutionary change in society is needed, where power is turned upside down and where for the first time in history, society is reorganised in the interests of the majority.

The mounting consequences of climate change, financial and economic disorder and war have led us to a crucial moment for the planet and its inhabitants. Humanity has arrived at an historical crossroads where we face key decisions. Our aim must be to extend the gains and advances that capitalism provides for a minority to all people in all countries through the development of a global society based on co-operation, co-ownership and sustainability. As *A House of Cards – from fantasy finance to global crash*, published by AWTW in 2007, explains:

> We are not, however, proposing to do away with all the structures of global corporations. Global networks, global systems for production and distribution and a global division of labour are advances for human society, though at present they serve profit-motivated corporate requirements. Many of the component parts of the system can be reused or recycled. We need to preserve these advances in a new global economy oriented towards the satisfaction of needs. Capitalism can and should be composted. Capitalism has developed an array of potentially useful methods and technologies. Once liberated from the straitjacket of profit and private ownership, these will form the basis of the sustainable society of the future.

49

The miners in 1984-5 found that they were unable on their own to save their jobs and their communities. Ultimately, the power to determine their futures rested with the state and capitalism. Today, new generations and other communities will, like the miners, rise to the challenge and create a leadership that sets its eyes on the main prize: the conquest of power. This is the way to prevent capitalism from turning another industry and its communities into a wasteland. The great miners' strike remains unfinished business.

The fight against pit closures
– the year in photographs

On the frontline

Police take over the streets around Cortonwood pit, November 1984

Miners lobbying the NUM headquarters in Sheffield learn from Arthur Scargill of the no-ballot decision, April 1984

Police cavalry charge at Orgreave, May 1984

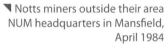
Notts miners outside their area NUM headquarters in Mansfield, April 1984

Orgreave, May 1984

Orgreave, May 1984

Picket at Yorkshire Main, near Doncaster, September 1984

Police cavalry charge at Denby Grange, near Wakefield

▲ Picketing a power station at the beginning of the strike, March 1984

◤ Mass Picket, Warsop Main, N Derbyshire, July 1984

▶ Orgreave, May 1984

▼ Woolley, Near Barnsley,
Yorkshire

◀ Police make an arrest,
Houghton Main, Yorkshire

▲ Pickets at Hunterston Docks are
numbered and photographed
after being arrested, Scotland,
May 1984

◥ Massive police escort for a
lone scab. Houghton Main,
Yorkshire, June 1984

▶ Police used increasingly
violent attacks to ensure scab
coal reached the Ravenscraig
steelworks. Hunterston
Docks, Scotland, May 1984

▲ Occupation at Whitwell pit. Those involved were sacked.

◥ Yorkshire Main, February 1985

▼ Orgreave, May 1984

◢ Orgreave

▲ Barricade Allerton Bywater

▼ Roadblock from Yorkshire into Notts, March 1984

Women's march in London, August 1984

▲ On the picket line at Cortonwood, January 1985

▼ Women`s march and rally in Barnsley, May 1984

◥ Women`s march and rally in Barnsley, May 1984

▶ March in Maerdy, South Wales, August 1984

▶ A miners`s wife makes her point to a strike-breaker, Rossington, July 1984

▼ Edlington women join the picket line at Yorkshire Main after marching to the pit, February 1985

Soup kitchen in Welbeck, Notts, November 1984

Xmas party for kids, Dodworth, Yorkshire, December 1984

Rossington soup kitchen towards
the end of the strike, February 1985

Rally in Barnsley, May 1984

▲ Kids meet Santa Claus at Frickley`s Xmas party

▼ Soup kitchen, Yorks, December 1984

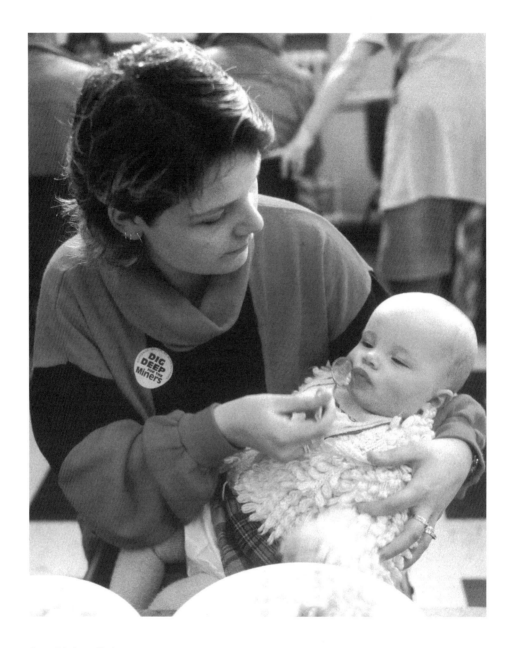

Soup kitchen, Yorks

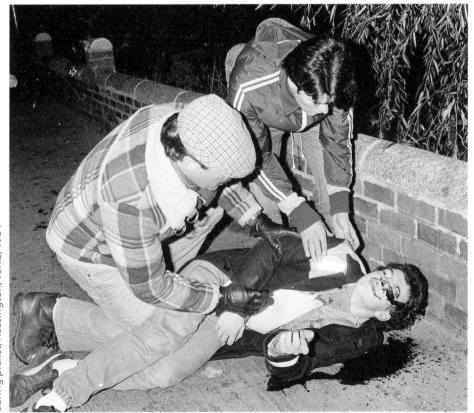

Darren Price seriously injured by police vehicle while standing on pavement during picket, Rossington, Yorks, 1984

Trevor Womersley, a young Hatfield striker, after being savagely beaten in a police attack at Brodsworth, October 1984

Funeral of David Gareth Jones, killed on the picket line at Ollerton, Notts, just a few days into the strike

Yorks miners shackled to a lamppost at a mass picket at Cresswell pit in North Derbyshire, July 1984

The 3 leaders of the NUM: Peter Heathfield, Mick McGahey, and Arthur Scargill at the TUC conference in September 1984

Scargill arrested at Orgreave, May 1984

Miners' march in London, February 1985

Rally in Barnsley, May 1984

Scenes from the huge
demonstration of 45,000
miners and supporters through
Mansfield, Notts in May 1984

▼ Edlington Women`s march,
February 1985

◄ Notts miners in the lobby of
the NUM delegates meeting in
Sheffield, April 1984

◀ Women`s rally in Barnsley, May 1984

▼ North-East miners on the march, May 1984

▲ Scottish miners march in London, February 1985   ▼ Return to work, Barrow Colliery, March 1985

March of 45,000 in the heart of the Notts coalfield, Mansfield, May 1984

Winding gear is broken up and re-cycled, Wales 1986

Closed pit, Durham, 1987

▲ The site of Cortonwood pit today - where the strike started in March 1984

▼ Steve Tulley, former NUM branch secretary, in front of derelict miners' houses, Frickley Colliery

Sources and references

The Miners Strike 1984-85 in Pictures by *News Line* photographers and reporters (New Park Publications)

The Enemy Within. MI5, Maxwell and the Scargill Affair by Seamus Milne (Verso)

Marching to the Faultline by Francis Beckett and David Hencke (Constable)

The Miners Strike: Loss without Limit by Martin Adeney and John Lloyd (Routledge and Keegan Paul)

The Story of David Gareth Jones by his father Mark Jones (New Park Publications)

The Enemies Within by Ian MacGregor with Rodney Tyler (Collins)

A World to Win by Paul Feldman and Corinna Lotz (Lupus Books)

Running a Temperature: an action plan for the eco-crisis by Penny Cole and Philip Wade (Lupus Books)

A House of Cards: from fantasy finance to global crash by Gerry Gold and Paul Feldman (Lupus Books)

Unmasking the State: a rough guide to real democracy by Paul Feldman (Lupus Books)

GB84 by David Peace (Faber and Faber)

The Shock Doctrine. The Rise of Disaster Capitalism by Naomi Klein (Allen Lane)

Daily blogs, campaigns, news and views

www.aworldtowin.net

a world to win

about A WORLD TO WIN

The global economic meltdown shows the urgent need to create a new democratic society based on co-ownership and co-operation in place of monopoly control and profit.

We campaign for A People's Charter for Democracy (see page 48) to end the rule of capitalist political and economic élites and guarantee basic human rights.

A World to Win aims to **inspire a revolutionary change** in society. We need your ideas and participation. Here's what you can do:

- visit our website
- sign the People's Charter for Democracy
- check out and comment on our daily blog
- write/make films/take photos for the website
- read our books
- come to a discussion meeting
- invite AWTW to speak to your organisation/friends/college
- join our movement

OUR BOOKS:

Unmasking the State – a rough guide to real democracy

A House of Cards – from fantasy finance to global crash
(free download)

Running a Temperature – an action plan for the eco-crisis
(free download)

A World to Win (purchase or free download)

Crash! - *new book about the global capitalist crisis - coming soon!*

CONTACT US AT:

www.aworldtowin.net • info@aworldtowin.net • 07871 745258
PO Box 942 London SW1V 2AR